Pe

First Guide

to

Clouds
and
Weather

John A. Day

Vincent J. Schaefer

HOUGHTON MIFFLIN COMPANY
BOSTON   NEW YORK

For information about permission to reproduce
selections from this book, write to
trade.permissions@hmhco.com or to Permissions,
Houghton Mifflin Harcourt Publishing Company,
3 Park Avenue, 19th Floor, New York, New York 10016.

PETERSON FIRST GUIDES,
PETERSON FIELD GUIDES and
PETERSON FIELD GUIDE SERIES
are registered trademarks of
Houghton Mifflin Harcourt Publishing Company.

Library of Congress Cataloging-in-Publication Data

Day, John A.
Peterson first guide to clouds and weather/
John A. Day, Vincent J. Schaefer.
p.   cm.
Includes index.
ISBN 978-0-395-90663-7
1. Clouds—Juvenile literature.
2. Weather—Juvenile literature.
I. Schaefer, Vincent J.   II. Title.
QC921.35.D38   1991
551.57′6—dc20   90-13379
CIP

Printed in China

SCP   35 34 33 32 31 30 29 28 27 26
4500711798

Editor's Note

In 1934, my *Field Guide to the Birds* first saw the light of day. That book was the first in the Peterson Field Guide Series, which has grown to over 40 volumes on a wide range of subjects, including *Field Guide to the Atmosphere.*

Even though the Field Guides are intended for both the novice and the expert, there are still many who would like something simpler to start with — a smaller guide to give them confidence. It is for this audience that the Peterson First Guides have been created.

The atmosphere, the subject of this book, is a part of nature that affects all of us every day. A dynamic sea of air that bathes all living things, it is essential to our well-being and even to our existence on this planet. The atmosphere, as such, cannot be seen, but its clouds are an ever-changing visual feast. Thus clouds naturally have become the major focus of this First Guide.

There is a slowly growing awareness that sun, Earth, ocean, air, and every living thing are parts of a vast ecological system. Thanks to transistors, computer chips, rockets, and other marvels of sense-expanding technology, we are starting to think and feel globally. A part of this awareness is the recognition that certain types of human activity can no longer be tolerated because they bring injury to the global ecological system.

The 1990s are a critical time for the welfare of our atmosphere. It is incumbent upon all of us to awake to the very real dangers that face the Earth and the skies if we do not incorporate sound ecological principles into our daily lives on all scales: personal, national, and global.

We hope that the *First Guide to Clouds and Weather* will contribute to your own awareness as you become better acquainted with the myriad cloud forms and full-color light shows that Mother Nature displays in her skies.

Roger Tory Peterson

Introducing the Clouds

Weather is a common denominator of life. It affects each of us every day, either directly or indirectly. Weather is more than just sun or rain. It is activity in the lower part of the atmosphere that results in wind, rain or snow, humidity, visibility, and clouds.

Most of the elements that help us forecast the weather are impossible to see directly. Wind, or the movement of the atmosphere over Earth's surface, is seen only in the fluttering of a flag or the rustling of leaves. It can be as gentle as a breeze or as destructive as a hurricane.

We cannot see humidity at all. We sense the degree of humidity by our personal comfort. We say, "It's hot and sticky today," or, "My skin feels dry."

Neither can we see air pressure, except as a reading on a barometer scale. We sense it only when we change elevation rapidly and our ears pop.

Clouds, of all the weather elements, can be easily seen and studied. They "float" by in the moving air, forming, growing, disappearing. They appear in a bewildering variety of forms. Some appear as thin filaments in the high sky. Others appear as ominous dark masses generating lightning bolts, thunder, torrential rain, and occasionally the dreaded, ropelike funnel of a tornado.

Because it is easiest to learn about things we can see, this book will deal first with clouds and then with the other aspects of weather. Before the days of media weather reports, people whose livelihood depended on the weather learned to make forecasts largely by observing clouds.

Most of this book is visual, with many pictures of clouds and optical effects such as rainbows and halos. These pictures are ordered so that a curious sky viewer can match what he or she sees with a picture and a description of that cloud type.

The last third of the book gives explanations of other weather elements: different kinds of precipitation, wind and air pressure, air masses and fronts, etc.

The information in this book can be used in two ways. First, we can try to forecast the weather. We can approach the sky as a scientist would, classifying the clouds by type and analyzing the likelihood of their producing precipitation. This is the practical value of this book — but there is another side to human nature.

We can also learn to appreciate the everyday sky: the majesty of a sunset, the pristine beauty of cirrus clouds, the pure radiance of a rainbow.

Astronauts, for example, are both analyzers and appreciators of the planet Earth. As scientists, they analyze data and act in logical ways on the basis of their analyses. Yet from their unique perspective in space, they have a chance to reflect on the human family living at the bottom of a sea of air, breathing in the life-giving oxygen and exhaling the carbon dioxide needed by trees and plants.

This rare telephotograph catches the green flash of the setting sun (see p. 66). The spherical shape of the sun is distorted by atmospheric refraction.

The sight of Earth from space — a blue-and-white orb shining against the deep blackness of outer space, a globe surrounded by a thin membrane of air — makes a profound impact on the consciousness of many astronauts. They realize that the ordinary air taken so much for granted by Earthlings is in fact extraordinary. They sense not only the beauty of Earth but the fragility of its atmosphere. The experience changes their lives.

Pictures of Earth taken from space have

This photo was taken from the space shuttle *Discovery* just before midnight on August 30, 1984. Note the silhouettes of a few large cumulonimbus clouds. The spacecraft was about 250 miles north-northeast of the Philippine Islands at an elevation of about 160 nautical miles.

heightened the awareness of millions of people around the globe. The beautiful photos have reminded us that we live in a very special place that needs our protection.

We who live out our lives at the bottom of the sea of air can also learn to appreciate Earth's special nature from our own unique perspective. Our hope is that this First Guide will serve both the analyzer and the appreciator in each of us.

WHO NAMED THE CLOUDS?
A HISTORICAL NOTE

Clouds held a particular fascination for a young Englishman named Luke Howard (1773–1864). His father had sent him to grammar school at Burford, a village some miles west of London. But Luke was more interested in the book of Nature than in volumes of the Greek and Latin classics.

Before 1800, observers spoke of clouds only as "essences" floating in the sky. Clouds had no names and were little understood. The nature and behavior of atmospheric gases, such as oxygen and nitrogen, were just being investigated in the laboratories of Great Britain and Europe.

In Luke Howard's school years, high-level dust from volcanic eruptions in Iceland and Japan caused lurid sunrises and sunsets. To Howard's logical young mind, clouds and complicated halos must be the result of cause and effect in the natural order. He wanted to know more.

At the age of 20, Howard returned to London to work as a pharmacist. As an avocation, he joined a group of scientists, known then as "natural philosophers," who called themselves the Askesians (searchers after knowledge). Each member, in turn, read a scientific paper to the others. Luke Howard's turn came one night during the winter of 1802–03. His paper was titled, "On the modification of clouds." In the language of today, *modification* means *classification*. It was so well received that it was published, and it has become a classic in the history of science. Today we still use the basic scheme Howard presented that night and the Latin names he assigned to the clouds.

Howard noted that there are three basic shapes of clouds: 1) heaps of separated cloud masses with flat bottoms and cauliflower tops, which he named cumulus (heap); 2) layers of cloud much wider than they are thick, like a blanket or mattress, which he named stratus (layer); and 3) wispy curls, like a child's hair, which he called cirrus (curl). To clouds generating precipitation he gave the name nimbus (rain).

Clouds are found in three shells, or layers, in the lower 10 miles of the atmosphere. These shells are called low (L), middle (M), and high (H). The table below summarizes the 12 major cloud types, by name and thickness, that have evolved from Howard's pioneering work.

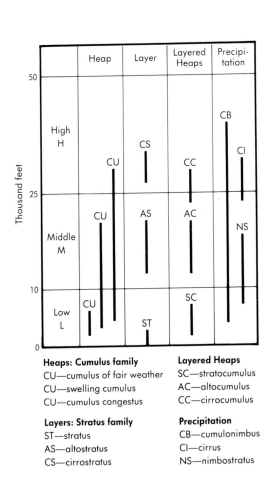

Heaps: Cumulus family
CU—cumulus of fair weather
CU—swelling cumulus
CU—cumulus congestus

Layers: Stratus family
ST—stratus
AS—altostratus
CS—cirrostratus

Layered Heaps
SC—stratocumulus
AC—altocumulus
CC—cirrocumulus

Precipitation
CB—cumulonimbus
CI—cirrus
NS—nimbostratus

HEAP CLOUDS

Fair-weather cumulus

Fair-weather cumulus clouds are low-level clouds that usually appear in late morning or early afternoon in settled weather. Surface air comes in contact with the sun-warmed earth, and the warmer "bubbles" of air rise into the atmosphere, where the water vapor in them eventually condenses. If moisture is evenly distributed horizontally through the air mass, the individual cloud bases are found at the same level, usually about 1500−4000 ft. (.5−1.5 km) in altitude.

The clouds are only a few hundred meters thick because the air mass is generally stable. Individual clouds are well separated by areas of descending air, where there are no clouds. The onset of condensation produces flattish bases, though glider pilots report bases are somewhat higher at the cloud center than around the edges.

Widely scattered puffs of cloud form over a plowed field.

Plentiful masses of fair-weather cumulus clouds have flat-tish bases and are not very tall.

Rows of cumulus clouds are called "cloud streets."

11

Swelling cumulus

Swelling cumulus clouds are formed in more energetic, unstable air masses, allowing the convection currents to rise to higher altitudes. Like fair-weather cumulus, they usually form in the late morning or early afternoon.

A growing cloud top has rounded, sharp-edged bumps, similar to a head of cauliflower. The clouds are substantially taller and have higher bases in the desert Southwest because it takes more lift to cool the ascending air to the dewpoint in the hot, dry climate. As with fair-weather cumulus, sinking air becomes warmer and dryer, causing the cloudless space around the clouds.

This large cloud mass was stimulated by air ascending over Mt. Hood in Oregon.

Swelling cumulus clouds have flat bases and growing towers.

An isolated heap of cloud pushes upward. The large cloud mass is made up of thousands of individual convection cells (see p. 84).

Cumulus congestus

Cumulus congestus is an extended development of swelling cumulus that forms in a still more energetic and unstable atmosphere. This cloud mass is made up of thousands of individual convection cells, all at different stages of their growth cycle. Each cell has a lifetime of about 10 minutes. The cloud mass contains many towers pushing up with great vigor.

The activity of cumulus congestus comes from the release of heat energy when vapor condenses to liquid. The still-growing top of the cloud is made of sharp-edged bumps, evidence that the mass has not turned into the ice of a cumulonimbus (precipitating) cloud, though some water droplets at the top may be supercooled.

Bases range from about 3000 to 6000 ft. (1–2 km) — 8000 to 12,000 ft. in the Southwest — with tops averaging about 16,000–33,000 ft. (5–10 km). Cloud color is usually white, though it can change to dark gray depending on the age of the cloud, the size of the cloud droplets, and the relative position of sun, cloud, and viewer.

The growth of this pure white cloud was stimulated by a rising column of hot air from a field burn below.

This very active cumulus congestus was photographed in late evening. The violent convection implies an unstable air mass.

A massive cumulus congestus cloud is marked by a high, flat base. Air that is very dry requires greater lift for condensation to begin.

LAYER CLOUDS

Stratus

Stratus is a layer cloud formation. Two features differentiate layer clouds from heap clouds. The first is that stratus are much wider and thinner. The second difference is the absence of rising and sinking air within layer clouds; they form when a layer of air is cooled to the saturation point. They are essentially featureless, with an ill-defined base and top.

A stratus cloud that lies on the ground is called ground fog. This kind of fog forms when the Earth's surface cools at night. Contact between the air and the cool surface lowers the air temperature to its dewpoint and brings about condensation. Cooling can also be accomplished by horizontal air movement over a colder surface, which produces advection fog, or by moist air ascending a gently sloping barrier, which produces upslope fog.

Ground fog is a stratus cloud that forms at ground level. It usually forms late at night or in the early morning hours. Cold, foggy air hugs the lowest elevations.

The Swiss Alps peek through formless stratus cloud.

Sea fog rolls into Tillamook Bay, Ore. Also known as advection fog, this is a stratus cloud with a low base.

Altostratus

Altostratus, or high stratus, occurs in the middle elevations between 10,000 and 20,000 ft. (3–6 km). It is primarily a cloud made of water droplets, not ice, though some of the water droplets may be supercooled. Generally gray in color because of the large size of the droplets, it often covers the entire sky and may be thick enough to obscure the sun. If the clouds are thin and ice crystals are present, the sun looks as it does when seen through a piece of ground glass.

Altostratus is formed primarily by the cooling resulting from gentle upglide over the surface of a warm front. It often is the forerunner of nimbostratus, from which steady precipitation falls.

The typical altostratus cloud may be about 1500–3000 ft. (.5–1 km) thick; the horizontal dimension may range from 60 to 600 mi. (100–1000 km). A single stratus cloud system can cover a whole state.

Sunlight is diffused through altostratus, as though seen through ground glass.

Dull gray layers of high *(alto)* stratus cloud (above and below) dim the sun.

Cirrostratus

Cirrostratus is composed of ice crystals and is generally found at high elevations above 20,000 ft. (6 km). It is like a veil with little or no structure, and usually covers a large area. From the ground it often appears thin, but pilots may describe it as an ice-crystal fog about 10,000 ft. (3 km) thick. It is generally milky white in color.

Cirrostratus usually results from cooling produced by ascent over the gently sloping boundary of a warm front.

Halos (see page 72) are frequently seen in cirrostratus clouds. When this happens it is an early warning of thickening and lowering clouds, with rain starting in 24 to 48 hours. The sun, when visible, always has a fuzzy outline..

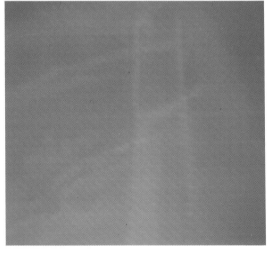

A very high layer of cirrostratus cloud of a uniform thickness covers the entire sky.

This slightly fibrous layer of ice-crystal cloud is milky white in color.

Cirrostratus cloud covers the sky behind Mont St. Michel in Normandy, France.

LAYERS AND HEAPS

Stratocumulus

Stratocumulus, as the name implies, is layered or stratified cumulus. This cloud forms when stable layers in the atmosphere slow down vertical motion, channeling it into horizontal development. The layered clouds show evidence of convection cells, producing thick and thin regions in the cloud that mark the rising and sinking motions, respectively, of the air. Stratocumulus and cumulus frequently are found together.

Stratocumulus clouds form in the lower part of the atmosphere. Their range of altitude is similar to that of fair-weather cumulus.

This cloudscape of both layers and heaps was photographed in New Mexico, very near the ranch where Georgia O'Keeffe captured the area's extraordinary light in her paintings.

A layer of stratus clouds over New Zealand mountains also contains some lumpy cumulus clouds.

The cloud heaps and spaces of blue sky in this layered cloud are evidence of convection.

Altocumulus

Altocumulus clouds are residents of the middle altitudes between 10,000 and 20,000 ft. (3–6 km). This high-layered heap cloud, one of the most pleasing to the eye, looks like a flock of sheep standing close together in a sky pasture. Each "sheep" corresponds to the upward motion of a convection cell. The spaces between sheep are regions of sinking air.

Altocumulus forms where there is ample moisture and unstable stratification bounded by a stable upper layer. The cloud can cover the entire sky or appear in smaller bands. It is sometimes called buttermilk sky. When seen in the early morning, such clouds often lead to thunderstorms by afternoon.

A relatively low-level altocumulus layer (about 10,000 ft.) shows randomly arranged convection cells. The thin spaces between cloud elements are regions of sinking air. The building shown is Josselin Castle in France.

A typical layer of altocumulus at 15,000 feet shows many individual convection cells.

The small convection cells of the altocumulus "mackerel sky" resemble fish scales.

Cirrocumulus

Cirrocumulus clouds are residents of the high region above 25,000 ft. (8 km). They are very-high-layered heaps. The convection cells are smaller than in altocumulus. Because of its resemblance to fish scales, the cirrocumulus is sometimes called mackerel sky. Cirrocumulus clouds seldom cover the entire sky, are often seen with cirrus clouds, and are often supercooled.

The presence of cirrocumulus indicates unstable air and the likelihood of rain later.

This cirrocumulus cloud layer lies at about 25,000 feet. It is primarily a water cloud, though some parts may have turned to ice and others may be supercooled.

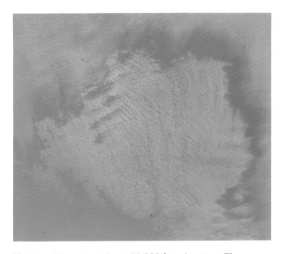

This cloud layer is at about 30,000 feet elevation. The convection cells appear small, partly because they are so far from Earth. Note the rifts, probably the result of natural cloud seeding by high ice crystals.

Adjacent layers of cirrocumulus are subject to rapid changes in the direction or speed of the wind, called shearing. This produces rows or billows of clouds.

PRECIPITATING CLOUDS

Nimbostratus

Nimbostratus is the cloud form that produces continuous rain or snow. It is a thick mass of cloud with no well-defined base, usually covering the whole sky. The color is dark gray. The lower edges may appear ragged. These ragged storm clouds are called scud.

Nimbostratus results from a mass of warm, moist air rising over the surface of a warm or occluded front. It can be widespread, covering an area of one or more states.

The beam from the lighthouse at Heceta Head, Ore., shines through a Pacific rainstorm.

Snow falls from widespread winter nimbostratus clouds.

Heavy clouds approaching from the ocean show the dark gray color, ragged edges, and steady rainfall typical of nimbostratus clouds.

Precipitating cumulus congestus

A precipitating cumulus congestus cloud is an active cumulus mass whose top has not yet reached the freezing level, yet which generates rain showers. This type of cloud is most frequently found over tropical oceans. It consists of many thousands of convection cells, and these are seen as the sharply defined cauliflower edges and tops. Each convection cell has a lifetime of just a few minutes. In active clouds like those shown here, a patient observer can watch the convection cells grow.

The base ranges from about 3500 to 7000 ft. (1–2 km) and the tops range from 20,000 to 33,000 ft. (6–10 km).

The crisply defined tops of this large precipitating cumulus cloud, which formed near Bermuda, show it is still a water cloud throughout. Showers are produced when water droplets collide and coalesce within the cloud mass.

Large cumulus congestus clouds form over the warm waters of the Indian Ocean. The clouds' bases are low because the air is very humid. Such clouds produce torrential rain but little lightning.

Precipitating cumulus congestus generate rain showers although the cloud's tops do not reach the freezing point. This photo, taken from an airplane, shows the outside edge of a huge storm cloud.

Cumulonimbus

Cumulonimbus is the most energetic of all the cumulus, or heap, family. It is made up of many thousands of individual convection cells. The top penetrates above the freezing level, where water droplets are transformed into ice crystals. This is seen as a change from the well-defined top of the cumulus congestus to a stringy form like spiky hair.

The cumulonimbus base ranges from about 3000 to 6000 ft. (1–2 km) — 8000 to 12,000 ft. in the Southwest — and, depending on the height of the freezing level, the top can be as low as about 16,000 ft. (5 km) to as high as about 65,000 ft. (20 km), penetrating into the stratosphere.

Heavy downpours of rain fall from the base of cumulonimbus clouds. In some conditions the precipitation may be in the form of the ice balls we call hail. In other conditions, lightning, with consequent thunder, discharges from cloud to ground or from cloud to cloud.

The top of this massive cloud reaches into the stratosphere, up to 60,000–70,000 feet. Its vertical motion is deflected outward by a "lid" of stable upper layers, producing the upper ring. Photo taken at Boulder, Colo.

Hail may be mixed with the rain falling from this active cumulonimbus mass.

The "fuzzy" top of this cumulonimbus cloud marks the transition from supercooled water to ice crystals and signals the onset of heavy showers.

Cumulonimbus, cont.

Lightning. A mature thundercloud develops a negative electric charge in its base and a positive charge in its top. Because like charges repel each other, the ground beneath the cloud becomes positively charged, resulting in a growing electrical field between cloud and ground. When the field exceeds three million volts per meter, the air begins to conduct electricity. The discharge of excess electrons from the cloud starts as a stepped leader. When the bolt approaches the ground, a very bright, hot return stroke surges up to the cloud, following the path of the stepped leader, as seen here.

Anvil cumulonimbus. These clouds form as the tremendous upward momentum of a cumulonimbus is deflected outward by the stable layer of the stratosphere, producing the anvil shape. Temperatures are low, and the clouds are a mixture of supercooled raindrops, cloud droplets, ice crystals, and snow.

Cirrus

Cirrus clouds consist of ice crystals. In temperate regions they are found at the highest levels, but in very cold weather they can even appear at the surface as fog. Cirrus clouds often appear with other cloud types, especially cirrocumulus.

Cirrus assumes many forms and patterns, but is generally hairlike (the Latin word *cirrus* means "curl") and fibrous. The color is milky white. Cirrus possesses an ethereal quality that makes it one of the most beautiful of all cloud forms.

The precipitation from cirrus is in the form of streams of ice crystals (snow), but the crystals usually evaporate in the warmer lower atmosphere.

Cirrus are tufted ice-crystal clouds. The ice crystals may precipitate in snow showers that evaporate in lower, warmer air.

The thick, fibrous plumes are dense streamers of falling ice crystals, or snow.

Streamers of ice crystals form at high elevations and then fall into air that is moving much faster, creating the curves.

UNUSUAL CLOUDS

Billow altocumulus. These low-level (about 10,000 ft.) clouds form as the result of shearing motion, changes in wind speed or direction that come with elevation. This produces compact, ropelike billows.

Billow altocumulus. Shearing generates rolls of ascending and descending air. Clouds occur in the ascending currents. Widely spaced billows (below) indicate active vertical growth and may generate a thunderstorm later in the day.

UNUSUAL CLOUDS, cont.

Banner. This cloud plume extends downwind from Mount Hood, Ore. Cooling due to falling air pressure may cause condensation when the air near the peak is very humid.

Cap. A well-formed cap cloud lies atop Mt. Shasta, Calif. The cloud generally remains stationary even as wind blows through it.

Mammato-cumulus. These clouds, called simply mamma by meteorologists, take the form of pouches of cold, cloudy air hanging from the underside of a cumulonimbus shelf. They frequently form under a thundercloud at the end of its life.

UNUSUAL CLOUDS, cont.

Lenticular altocumulus. The name means "lens-shaped," but these clouds look startlingly like flying saucers. They form at the crest of a wave in the airstream caused by a mountain peak or ridge. The remarkably symmetrical cloud above formed in the lee of Mt. St. Helens, Wash. The one below is an example of the double-layered cloud that forms near Mt. Washington, N.H. It sometimes resembles a stack of flapjacks.

Lenticular altocumulus. Like cap clouds, lenticular clouds remain stationary while winds blow through them. The cloud above, photographed in New Zealand, has a less well-rounded but still distinctive shape — this cloud was dubbed "Woody Woodpecker." The smooth clouds below formed in the lee of the Sierra Nevadas.

43

Pileus. A large cloud mass can have much the same effect as a mountain peak when winds flow over the top; a cap cloud called pileus can form when a moist current of air is forced over a growing cumulus cloud. Winds blow through pileus clouds.

Steam fog forms over a relatively warm lake surface in the early morning. Evaporation saturates the air, producing condensation (fog). The fog evaporates when it mixes with the drier air at higher levels.

Sea smoke. Transitory patches of fog form when colder air flows over a warmer water surface. This photo of the sea surface was taken from the air.

UNUSUAL CLOUDS, cont.

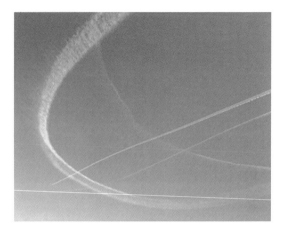

Contrails form in the wake of aircraft, the result of condensation of moisture added to the air by the burning of fuel. Above, the most recent trails are still straight; older ones have been curved and spread by wind. The spreading, crossed trails below indicate high humidity at that elevation.

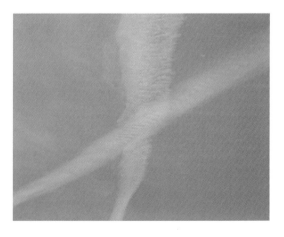

Snow showers develop from contrails. The streams of ice crystals evaporate in the lower layers, which are warmer and drier.

This contrail developed pendules, or elements of sinking air akin to mammato-cumulus (see p. 41).

Iridescence. Pale shades of pink, blue, and green are caused by diffraction in high clouds composed of particles of slightly different sizes.

Noctilucent cloud. These "luminous night clouds" are made of water frozen on meteoric dust found at the top of the atmosphere (about 50 miles up). They are seen, rarely, at twilight or dawn. Photo taken in Turku, Finland.

Crepuscular rays. The term means "rays at twilight," though they may also be seen at dawn. The impact of the sun's rays on foreign particles in the air makes the rays visible as shafts of white light. The convergence of the shafts is an illusion of perspective, like the convergence of railroad tracks.

UNUSUAL CLOUDS, cont.

Parhelia. This rarely seen portion of a 22° halo (see p. 72) is produced by refraction in hexagonal ice crystals, which oscillate as they fall. Note that the inner color is red.

Virga is falling precipitation, usually frozen, that evaporates before it reaches the ground. This curtain of virga formed over Navajo country in Arizona.

CLOUDS ON WEATHER RADAR

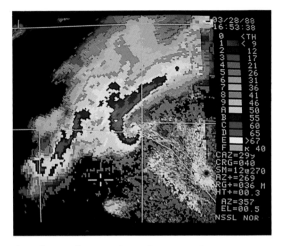

The red areas of this weather radar picture show an intense "precipitation echo" in the southwest sector of a storm. This usually means a tornado is forming. (Norman, Okla.; March 28, 1988.)

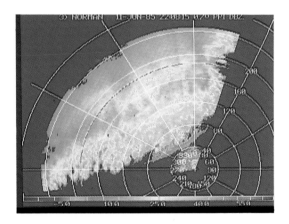

National Severe Storms Laboratory radar shows an approaching squall line of thunderstorms. (Norman, Okla.; June 10, 1985.)

SEVERE WEATHER CLOUDS

Hurricane. The orbiter *Apollo 7* took this portrait of Hurricane Gladys over the Gulf of Mexico on October 17, 1968. The cumulonimbus bands spiraling into the center are quite clearly shown.

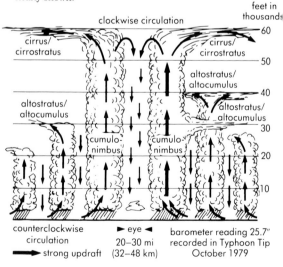

Cross section of the eye of a hurricane.

Tornado. A funnel cloud drops from a ring of cloud protruding from the base of an intense cumulonimbus. It is opaque because of the condensation of surrounding air as it is sucked into the low-pressure vortex, then expands and cools. This tornado was photographed at Osnabrock, N.D., on July 29, 1978.

Waterspout. A waterspout is a tornado that forms over water. The one above was photographed over the Florida Keys on September 10, 1969. Note that the large funnel includes three individual vortexes.

CLOUDS FROM ALOFT

At 25,000 feet, altocumulus seen from a jet resemble strato-cumulus.

This cloudscape is composed of cumulus towers with anvil cumulonimbus in the left background.

Scattered cumulus clouds are seen from a flight level of about 35,000 feet.

From about 40,000 feet up, we are looking straight down onto the top of a towering cumulus congestus on its way to producing a thunderstorm. The cauliflower appearance is evidence of extreme turbulence.

CLOUDS FROM ALOFT, cont.

Clouds near Hawaii show great variety in size, from little puffs to mature thunderstorms. Oceanic clouds are effective rainmakers.

Active convection leads to a mass of swelling cumulus in the foreground. Fair-weather cumulus can be seen in the distance.

These large waves of cloud, or "rollers," were formed by shearing motion, or changes in wind speed and direction, atop a deck of stratus clouds.

A view of the Canary Islands taken from an altitude of 160 nautical miles shows vigorous convective activity. This photo was taken during a 1989 mission of the shuttle *Discovery*.

A line of high-based swelling cumulus form over Chicago at the south end of Lake Michigan.

Very large cumulonimbus form along the African Intertropical Front. This photo was taken with a large-format camera from the shuttle *Atlantis* in 1989, 160 nautical miles above the Ivory Coast.

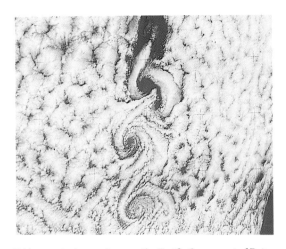

Eddies in stratocumulus over the Pacific Ocean west of Baja California were photographed from *Skylab 3* in 1973. The Isla de Guadalupe, seen at top, presents an obstacle to the prevailing northerly winds, and clouds produced by a cold current running south are prevented from rising by dominant high pressure over the Pacific. The vortex is a permanent feature of the area.

The view from space station *Skylab* shows turbulent eddies alongside the Yucatan current in the Caribbean Sea, June 1973. These eddies, unknown before they were photographed from *Skylab*, are 10–40 miles wide, with depths greater than 300 feet. There are clear skies over the eddies, with towering cumulus over the warm current boundary.

Color in the Sky

Why is the sky blue?

Seen from outside Earth's atmosphere, in outer space, the sky has no color. The deep blackness of space is interrupted only by pinpoints of light from distant stars and an intense source of white light coming from the nearest star, 93 million miles distant — our sun.

Sky color results from an interaction between air molecules and solar radiation in which air molecules momentarily absorb solar energy, then scatter it in all directions.

The energy of blue scattered light is about 16 times greater than that of red scattered light. When we look at the sky, our eye collects light of all wavelengths. But the eye is overwhelmed by the more energetic blue light, and the mind pronounces, "The sky is blue."

A deep blue sky is framed by hooked cirrus clouds and fair-weather cumulus.

What makes the setting sun red?

Earth's sun is a white star, hotter than red stars and cooler than blue stars. The word *white* means a balance of energy across a wide range of wavelengths. When Isaac Newton passed white light through a prism, he demonstrated that it consists of a spectrum of different colors.

The sun looks red at sunset because Earth's atmosphere is not clean. The lower portions contain many tiny foreign particles up to several microns across (1 micron = one-millionth of a meter). When the sun lies low in the sky, its beams pass through a longer path of "dirty" air than when it is straight overhead. The larger particles scatter and absorb blue light out of the beam, so the sun looks red. The sun is usually redder at sunset than at sunrise because the atmosphere is less disturbed at dawn. A red sun can be seen at midday only at times of severe pollution, such as that caused by a forest fire.

The pristine blue of the sky also disappears in heavy pollution. The scattered blue light is partially absorbed by the larger pollution particles, leaving a dirty gray. In many cities around the world, the sky is no longer blue.

The haze of a prairie fire reddens the low-lying sun.

COLOR IN THE SKY, cont.

Sunrise

Sunrise just south of Mt. Hood, Ore.

The rising sun turns silver the edges of a mass of cumulus cloud.

Sunset

Evening sky behind the domes of St. Peter and St. Paul, Salzburg, Austria.

The rays of the setting sun illuminate the undersurface of a cumulonimbus cloud shelf.

COLOR IN THE SKY, cont.

The silhouettes of cloud forms appear against the darkening sky as the sun drops below the horizon.

The colors in this sunset range from yellow through orange to violet.

Contrails left in the high atmosphere by a Minuteman missile fired from Vandenberg A.F.B., Calif., are still illuminated after sunset.

A momentary green flash was seen immediately after the sun's disk disappeared below the sharply defined horizon (see p. 66).

COLOR IN THE SKY, cont.

The Green Flash

A dazzling emerald-green color is sometimes seen just after the red rim of the sun disappears below a sharply defined horizon. This is a result of refraction, or bending of light rays, as they pass through layers of different air density.

Because of this bending, the sun's image is refracted upward by one diameter (see illustration). Since green light is bent more than red, the green image lies slightly above the red image, and 1.4 seconds after the red sun sets a green image appears. This is known as the "green spot."

The more rare "green flash," which lasts about two seconds, is caused by the channeling and focusing effects of cooler layers of air settling close to the warmer air in contact with a warmer water surface — a complex situation.

Not many people have seen the green flash. It does not occur at every sunset, even when the atmosphere is clear.

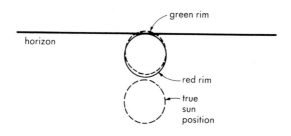

The "green flash" occasionally seen at sunset is caused by atmospheric refraction.

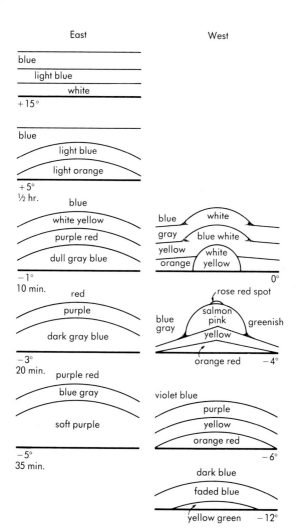

East   West

blue
light blue
white
+15°

blue
light blue
light orange
+5°
½ hr.

blue
white yellow
purple red
dull gray blue
−1°
10 min.

blue white
gray blue white
yellow white
orange yellow
0°

red
purple
dark gray blue
−3°
20 min.

rose red spot
salmon pink
blue gray greenish
yellow
orange red −4°

purple red
blue gray
soft purple
−5°
35 min.

violet blue
purple
yellow
orange red
−6°

dark blue
faded blue
yellow green −12°

Sky colors at sunrise and sunset (for clean air). Numbers give height and time of sun above and below the horizon.

COLOR IN THE SKY, cont.

Rainbows

When the sun's rays encounter a spherical
water drop, most of the light passes through
the central portion of the drop. Rainbows,
however, are produced by the light that passes
through the extreme upper and lower portions
of the drop. The top illustration shows such

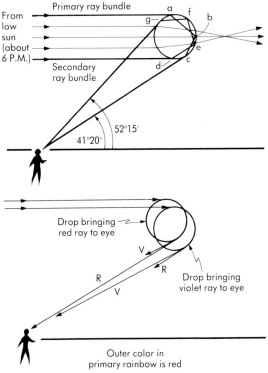

Outer color in
primary rainbow is red

Sometimes two rainbows are visible: when the sun's rays
pass through a raindrop *(top)*, the rays striking the upper
edge of the drop form the primary bow, and rays striking the
lower edge form the secondary bow. *Bottom:* The observer
sees violet light, which is most bent by refraction, coming
from a raindrop lower in the sky than the drop that sends
red light. So violet is the interior color of the primary bow,
red of the secondary bow.

"bundles of rays." The bundle entering the upper edge of the drop is bent by refraction as it enters the drop at *a*. It strikes the interior surface at *b* at an angle so great that it is completely reflected, striking the drop's inner surface at *c*, and emerges bent by refraction from its original direction by nearly 139°.

The bundle shown entering the lower edge of the drop at *d* is reflected twice, at *e* and *f*, and is refracted when it emerges at *g*. These are the two particular bundles that come to the observer's eye to produce the primary and secondary bows, respectively.

As shown in the illustration at lower left, violet light is bent slightly more than red on refraction. This means that the violet light ray will change direction a bit more than 139° and the red ray a bit less. Therefore the vertical angle of these rays, measured from the horizon, will be a little less than 41° for the violet and a little more than 41° for the red.

A gull intersects a primary rainbow.

Rainbows, cont.

The figure below shows a sheet of raindrops illuminated by the sun's rays at sunset parallel to Earth's surface. Light arriving at the eye of the observer will come only from drops arrayed about the periphery of two cones, one whose vertical angle is 41° and another whose angle is 52°. A viewer standing with his back to the sun and holding an imaginary conical paper drinking cup to his eye, as shown in the illustration, can predict where the rainbow will appear in the sky at any time of day.

A full half-bow will be seen only at 6 A.M. and 6 P.M. At noon there will be no visible bow unless the viewer is in an airplane or on a mountaintop looking down, in which case a 360° circle could be seen. Showers are more frequent in the late afternoon than in the early morning; rainbows are more frequent in the afternoon for this reason.

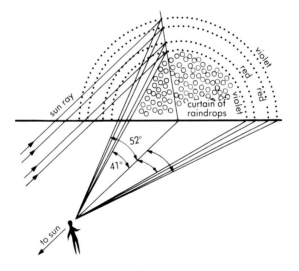

Light rays from the rainbow come to an observer's eye along the surface of an imaginary cone, the axis of which extends from the sun to the observer to the center of the bow. When the sun's rays are horizontal, a 180° bow is visible.

The primary bow is red on the outside and violet on the inside. The colors are reversed in the secondary bow.

This primary bow shows supernumerary inner bows. These may appear when the raindrops are uniform in size.

COLOR IN THE SKY, cont.

Halos

Several kinds of halos are caused by the presence of ice crystals in cirrostratus clouds between an observer and the sun or moon.

The most commmon halo is the small, or 22° halo, which appears in the presence of a veil of clouds and its hexagonal ice-crystal prisms of uniform size. These are found at temperatures below approximately − 15°C. A hexagonal prism is essentially two 60° triangles, laid base to base, with truncated tips. The angle of bending from a straight line is 22°, with the angle slightly greater for violet light than for red. As a result, we see a colored ring around the sun or moon with red on the inside, surrounded by yellow, then green, and with blue-violet on the outside.

If the arm is outstretched, the 22° angle of the small halo is approximately the same as that measured by the outspread hand from thumb to little finger.

The halo, a portion of which is visible at the top of the photo, formed by refraction in the hexagonal ice crystals of a cirrostratus cloud. Block the sun's disk while observing or photographing halos to avoid eye damage.

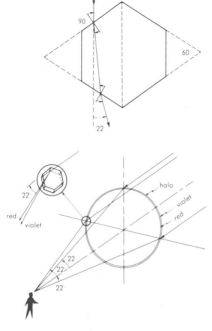

Light rays are bent by an angle of 22°; violet light is bent a bit more, red a bit less. Ice crystals high in the atmosphere fall in random orientation. Those that bring light rays to convergence at the observer's eye produce the 22° halo. Violet light comes from crystals slightly farther removed from the sun-observer line.

A tangential arc curves upward from the top of this unusual halo.

73

COLOR IN THE SKY, cont.

Coronas

The corona is seen when the light from the moon (or sun) shines through a thin layer of high water-droplet clouds. In its simplest form, the corona appears as a colored disk surrounding the sun or moon whose border is bluish, merging into yellowish white, with a brownish outer edge at a width of one or more moon (or sun) diameters.

The corona is the result of light bending by diffraction in the presence of small, spherical water droplets and ice crystals in high clouds. The more uniform the size of the droplets, the purer the colors in the corona. The smaller the cloud droplets, the larger the corona diameter. Young clouds such as those found in thin altostratus are the best corona producers, since they have very uniform droplets. In older clouds the ring diameters overlap and the colors are weaker.

The full moon is surrounded by three repeating rings of color resulting from the interaction of diffracted light and water droplets of uniform size. Red light is on the outside of the ring.

This lunar corona was photographed in eastern New York on a cold winter night.

Aurora borealis. The neon colors of the northern lights are the result of radiation given off in the very high atmosphere by molecules that are energized by particles from the sun, or solar wind.

COLOR IN THE SKY, cont.

Sun pillar. A beam, or pillar, of sunlight is reflected upward from the horizontal surfaces of hexagonal ice crystals.

Sun dog. When the sun, an observer, and horizontal surfaces of ice plates are in the same plane, refraction produces bright spots on both sides of the sun at 22°. These are also called mock suns.

Heiligenschein. A diffuse white ring is seen here surrounding the shadow of an object on a dew-covered lawn when the sun is low. The effect is caused by diffraction and by reflecton on the surfaces of water drops.

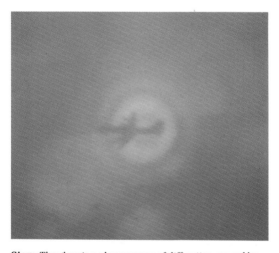

Glory. The glory is a phenomenon of diffraction caused by the presence of very small water droplets, yielding a bright ring of colors around an object's shadow. As you observe a glory, you may see the diameter change as a result of a change in the size of the water droplets. The larger the glory, the smaller the droplets.

Precipitation

THE WATER CYCLE

Water moves from Earth to the atmosphere and back again in an endless, global cycle. Evaporation from oceans, lakes, and rivers and transpiration from trees and plants add water vapor to the atmosphere, leading to cloud formation and precipitation. The rain and snow flows directly to the ocean via streams and rivers or is stored underground and flows oceanward more slowly.

ANVIL CUMULONIMBUS

UPDRAFT

DOWNDRAFT

CUMULONIMBUS

CL

P

GW

R

KEY

CL: Condensation level
 E: Evaporation
 T: Transpiration
 R: Run-off—rivers
 P: Precipitation
GW: Ground water

WATER, MIRACLE SUBSTANCE

Two atoms of the most plentiful element in the universe, hydrogen, combine with oxygen to make H_2O — water. Eighty percent of Earth's surface is covered by water. We are like fish living at the bottom of a sea of watery air.

If water behaved like any other substance, Earth would be radically different, and we would not be here to observe it. Below are a few of the ways that water is unique:

• Water is the only substance commonly found on Earth in all its three states simultaneously: gas, liquid, and solid.

• Water conserves heat extremely well compared to other substances such as soil. The vast amount of water in the oceans moderates Earth's climate, preventing wild swings between hot and cold.

• Water releases unusually large amounts of heat energy when it condenses or freezes. Conversely, water uses large amounts of heat energy when it melts or evaporates.

• Water is the only substance that is less dense in its solid form than in its liquid form. One effect of this anomaly is that fish can live under the ice floating on lake surfaces in winter.

• Water is the universal solvent. This means that nearly everything, given enough time, will dissolve in water. It is the reason that your blood can carry nutrients throughout your body.

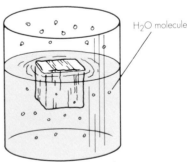

H_2O molecule

Ice floats because water is less dense in its solid form than in its liquid form.

IMPORTANCE OF PRECIPITATION

The importance of precipitation to life on Earth cannot be overstated. This is a water planet, and we are water beings. Without adequate rainfall and snowfall the land masses of Earth would become vast deserts. Such deserts already exist in several places around the globe. Some of them are growing larger, as in the Sahel, the southern boundary of the Sahara Desert. Without rainfall adequate for farming, the drought and starvation seen in Ethiopia and Sudan in recent years would be worldwide.

Rainfall also cleans the air of pollutants. Small particles of pollutants and chemical compounds (ions) attach to the falling drops and are carried to Earth. An unfortunate result of this process is acid rain.

Although precipitation almost never falls in the absence of a cloud, not every cloud generates precipitation. Several processes are involved in the formation of precipitation. A useful tool for remembering the several steps leading to precipitation is the Precipitation Ladder. The rungs become our steps. To get to the top of the ladder (precipitation), each step must be taken in turn. We will begin climbing the Precipitation Ladder on page 82.

THE PRECIPITATION LADDER

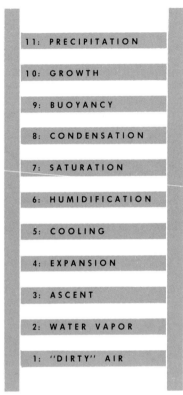

11: PRECIPITATION

10: GROWTH

9: BUOYANCY

8: CONDENSATION

7: SATURATION

6: HUMIDIFICATION

5: COOLING

4: EXPANSION

3: ASCENT

2: WATER VAPOR

1: "DIRTY" AIR

Step 1: "Dirty" Air

Air is a mixture of several gases continually
blended by stirring in the atmosphere. Fortunately, air is not "clean" — it also contains
tiny particles of solid matter. If it weren't for
these particles of "dirt," there would be no
clouds at all.

The particles on which water vapor molecules gather are called cloud condensation nuclei. They consist principally of certain dust
and salt particles. These nuclei are one of the
two prerequisites for cloud formation.

Step 2: Water Vapor

The other necessary factor in cloud formation is water in its gaseous form, or water vapor. Water vapor is but one of the gases that make up air. Like the others, it exerts its own pressure, which is about $\frac{1}{100}$ of the total air pressure. The amount of water vapor varies from place to place and from time to time, unlike other gases such as oxygen and nitrogen, which are always present in the same fixed proportions.

The maximum amount of water vapor is limited by the temperature. When it is very cold, water vapor exerts only $\frac{1}{500}$ of the total air pressure; when it is very hot, it can (but might not) exert up to $\frac{1}{25}$ of the total air pressure.

An easy, though simplistic, way to think of the water molecule is as a shape similar to Mickey Mouse's head, with its two atoms of hydrogen and one of oxygen (H_2O). A more realistic portrayal of a water molecule is also shown below.

Water vapor carries vast amounts of energy. It is the "fuel" that propels the atmosphere.

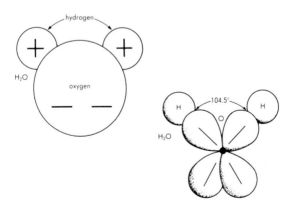

Two models of a water molecule: the model on the right is more realistic.

Step 3: Ascent

Thanks to the tug of gravity, air does not escape into space, and most air movement is channeled into horizontal directions. Four sets of circumstances lead to short-lived vertical motions:

- Convection takes place when lighter, less dense air moves upward and is replaced by heavier, denser air. If you have ever watched a pot of water coming to a boil, you have seen convection cells in action. The water that comes in contact with the bottom of the pan is warmed, then rises and is replaced by cooler water, circulating until the water comes to a "rolling boil."
- Sometimes too many competing air currents try to squeeze into the same space at the same time, just as too many cars may try to merge onto the same road. Squeezing in the horizontal flow, known as convergence, creates a compensatory vertical motion.
- Physical barriers such as hills or mountains can force air to rise. This is called orographic lift.
- Colder air is denser than warm air (that is, cold air has more mass per unit volume). Air of greater density hugs closest to the surface. Therefore, a mass of warmer air is displaced abruptly at the leading edge of cold, dense air, as in the case of a cold front, and a mass of warmer air glides smoothly over a retreating mass of cool air, as in the case of a warm front.

warmer (lighter)   cooler   warmer

Convection cells

Orographic lift

cold air mass

warm air mass

NS   AS   CS

warm
air
mass

cool air mass

Three methods by which air rises: convection, orographic lift, and fronts. A fourth method is called convergence.

Step 4: Expansion

Air is most dense at sea level, for it is there that its molecules are packed closest together. Air pressure drops rapidly with elevation.

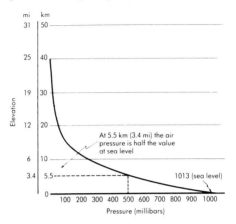

At 5.5 km (3.4 mi) the air pressure is half the value at sea level

1013 (sea level)

Pressure (millibars)

Visualize a balloon filled with air molecules, as shown in the illustration below, being released and then rising into the sky. As the balloon rises from sea level, the air pressure around it drops. The balloon will continuously expand in order to balance the interior and exterior pressure on its walls.

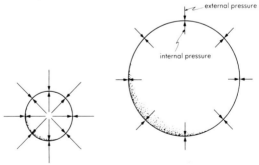

external pressure

internal pressure

Step 5: Cooling

Why does air get cooler when it rises? Picture the balloon getting larger as it rises. Each air molecule hits the wall and bounces back, pushing the walls outward. This pushing uses energy. Since air molecules have no access to external sources of energy, they use energy from the speed of their molecular motion, or kinetic energy. Molecules are more active at high temperatures than they are at low temperatures. When kinetic energy decreases, the temperature of the air drops. This is called adiabatic change.

Adiabatic cooling is the cause of most of our clouds and weather. Air temperature drops by about 5.5°F for every 1000 feet of ascent (1°C/100 m). By the same process, sinking air is compressed and warmed at the same rate.

Step 6: Humidification

Humidification is the increase of the relative humidity of the air. Relative humidity expresses the relationship of three factors: the actual amount of water vapor present in the air, the amount of water vapor that could be present at that temperature, and the tempera-

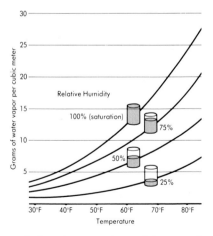

The graph shows how many grams of gaseous water can be found in a cubic meter of air at different temperatures. High temperatures permit much more water than low temperatures.

ture itself. Relative humidity is the amount of water vapor in the air expressed as a percentage of the maximum amount possible at that temperature.

If the relative humidity is 80 percent, for example, the air holds 80 percent of the moisture that is possible at that temperature.

Cooling is the most important method of humidification. Remember that temperature drops quickly as air rises, 1°C for every 100 meters of ascent. Warm air allows for more water vapor than cool air, so when air cools, the relative humidity goes up.

A second way of increasing relative humidity is by increasing the actual amount of moisture in the air. This happens when water evaporates from liquid sources, such as oceans, lakes, and even raindrops.

Step 7: Saturation

When the relative humidity reaches 100 percent, the air is said to be saturated. Cool air reaches 100 percent humidity, or "saturation," while holding much less water vapor than warm air, as seen in the table on p. 87.

Step 8: Condensation

Beyond saturation, additional water vapor will produce supersaturation, or a relative humidity over 100 percent. Nature then looks for "landing sites" for additional water molecules.

These landing sites are found in the small particles called cloud condensation nuclei, principally tiny motes of salt or dust (see Step 1).

Salt particles may enter the atmosphere through breaking wave action or from air bubbles bursting at the surface of the sea. They love water so much that they start to attract water molecules at humidities as low as 80%. This causes the common haziness along coastlines, and it is also the reason that salt is so hard to get out of the shaker in humid weather.

Other particles, such as bits of claylike dust, perhaps abraded by wind from the plateaus of Mongolia, start to take on water molecules at 100% relative humidity. When gaseous water molecules accumulate about the nuclei, condensation is taking place. The volume of a cloud droplet is one million times that of its condensation nucleus.

Step 9: Buoyancy

Evidence of the principle of buoyancy is all around us. Ice floats on the surface of water, as does wood; a helium-filled balloon rises when released; hot gases rise from a smoke-stack. In general, lighter, less dense substances are displaced upward by heavier, denser substances. Centuries ago, Archimedes first explained this principle of buoyancy, or how air can move upward against the pull of gravity.

When a hot-air balloon begins to sink, the balloonist burns fuel to raise the temperature of the air in the balloon. Its buoyancy is increased, and the balloon rises.

During condensation, water vapor releases its heat energy, or latent heat, as it changes from a gas to a liquid. The latent heat of water is unusually large compared to other substances, nearly 600 calories per gram. More latent heat released adds buoyancy to the rising air, contributing to its ascent.

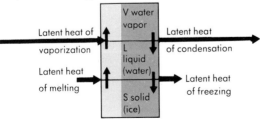

S→L melting   L→V evaporation   V→L condensation   L→S freezing

Water gives off large amounts of energy, or latent heat, when it changes from a gas to a liquid or from liquid to ice. Conversely, water *uses* large amounts of energy when it changes from ice to liquid or from liquid to gas.

Step 10: Growth

There are three ways by which cloud droplets grow to a size large enough to fall from the cloud as precipitation:

- By direct deposition of water molecules on the surfaces of cloud droplets. This is a very slow process.
- Larger drops fall faster than smaller ones. This means that larger drops will collide with smaller ones as they fall. Not every collision results in a joining; sometimes the smaller drop bounces off the larger one. The size ratio most likely to result in coalescence is 1 to .6; that is, the smaller drop has a diameter .6 times that of the larger. This process happens more rapidly when the cloud is made up of droplets of different sizes. Growth is enhanced in clouds in which there is an updraft, such as the cumulus, because the droplets stay in the clouds longer.
- Water has the ability to stay liquid at temperatures as cold as $-40°C$ or F (the Celsius and Fahrenheit scales cross at $-40°$). This is called supercooling. When the temperature in a cloud is below freezing, it may contain small ice crystals and supercooled water droplets. When a supercooled water droplet and an ice crystal are near neighbors, the ice crystal receives water molecules from the evaporating water droplet. In time, the water droplet disappears, and the ice crystal grows. At temperatures around $-10°C$, these crystals develop branches or arms, and they join arms with others as they fall. This is the origin of snowflakes.

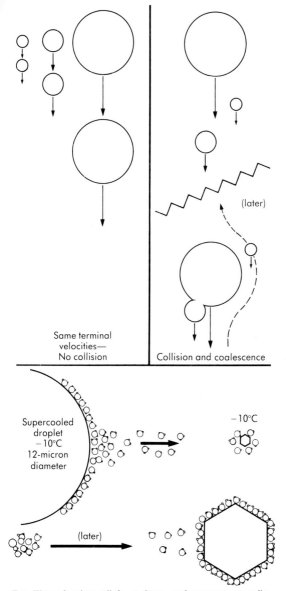

Same terminal velocities—No collision

Collision and coalescence

(later)

Supercooled droplet −10°C 12-micron diameter

−10°C

(later)

Top: Water droplets collide, coalesce, and grow more rapidly if the cloud is made up of droplets of different sizes. *Bottom:* Snowflakes grow when an ice crystal scavenges water from an adjacent evaporating supercooled water droplet.

Step 11. Precipitation

The table below shows the sizes of various water particles. Notice that a drop of drizzle has a volume one million times larger than that of a cloud droplet. Clouds generate precipitation only when the cloud droplets have increased in volume by a million times or more.

Precipitation can be divided into 100 or more types. We will describe several of the main categories on the following pages.

| Typical Particle | Diameter | | Volume Relative to |
	microns	millimeters	That of a Cloud Droplet
Cloud nucleus	0.12	0.00012	1/1,000,000
Cloud droplet	12	0.012	1
Large droplet	100	0.1	579/1
Mist	500	0.5	72,300/1
Drizzle drop	1200	1.2	1,000,000/1
Raindrop	3000	3.0	15,600,000/1
Heavy shower drop	6000	6.0	125,000,000/1

Note that a drop of drizzle has a volume one million times larger than that of a cloud droplet, and that the volume of a cloud droplet is one million times that of a cloud condensation nucleus.

"Down the ladder"

When air sinks, it goes "down the ladder," and the sequence of events is reversed. Raindrops and cloud droplets evaporate.

Descent results in compression of air. The energy used in compression produces adiabatic heating at the rate of 1°C for every 100 meters of descent.

CLOUD SEEDING

In 1946, Dr. Vincent Schaefer, then at the General Electric research labs, made a serendipitous discovery. He was able to transform a supercooled cloud (formed in a deep freeze) to ice crystals using tiny grains of dry ice. The evaporating dry ice caused intense local cooling below a "magic number" of $-40°F$ ($-40°$ C). This brought about the spontaneous creation of large numbers of ice crystals from water vapor, which proceeded to scavenge water from the neighboring cloud droplets and fall as snow.

Dry-ice cloud seeding is useful in clearing supercooled fog droplets from fog-bound airports in winter. These conditions often occur in Salt Lake City, for example.

Also in 1946, Dr. Bernard Vonnegut found that submicroscopic crystals of silver iodide could transform supercooled clouds to ice. This is the agent primarily used in cloud seeding today, and can enhance winter snow pack by at least 10 percent along mountain ranges such as the Oregon and Washington Cascades and the California Sierra Nevada. More snow pack results in more water available for summer irrigation in those areas.

This photo was taken 24 minutes after a solid cloud deck was seeded with 75 pounds of crushed dry ice.

TYPES OF LIQUID PRECIPITATION

Raindrops vary in size and shape, depending on the type of cloud from which they fall and the intensity of the air movement in the cloud. Small raindrops are spherical in shape. As they get larger they take on a flattened shape, somewhat like a hamburger bun, from the effects of air friction.

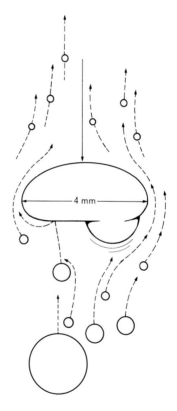

A large raindrop assumes the shape of a hamburger bun because of the effect of air friction. If you could ride on the large drop, you would see smaller droplets moving around you in the airstream, just as insects may move past the windshield of a moving car. Some smaller drops bounce off the larger one; some coalesce with it.

Contrary to common TV-weather graphics, raindrops are not teardrop-shaped. This myth probably had its origin in the shape taken by water at the moment it drips from a faucet.

The following types of liquid precipitation are arranged by size, starting with the largest

Showers. Raindrops that fall in showers from an active heap cloud such as a cumulus congestus or cumulonimbus are large, up to 6 mm in diameter, with a wide range of smaller sizes included.

Rain. Raindrops that fall steadily from a layered cloud such as a nimbostratus are relatively uniform in size, ranging from 1−2 mm in diameter.

Drizzle. Composed of uniform, small drops about .2−.5 mm in diameter, falling out of stratus clouds. This type of precipitation soaks into the ground quite effectively to depths of .1−.5 cm per hour.

Mist. Small raindrops that fall from stratus clouds range in diameter from .05−.8 mm. These are sometimes called Oregon mist or Scotch mist.

TYPES OF SOLID PRECIPITATION

Solid forms of precipitation are more readily observed than liquid forms. The variety is quite remarkable, including some less familiar varieties such as graupel.

If you live in a region where snow rarely reaches the ground, you can still see snow by looking up at the sky: cirrus clouds are composed of ice crystals; the upper portions of shafts of heavy precipitation generally consist of snow, graupel, or hail. Much of this solid

Types of Solid Precipitation

Graphic symbol	Typical forms			
⬡				Plates
✳				Stellars
▭				Columns
← →				Needles
⊕				Spatial dendrites
⊢⊣				Capped columns
✕◠				Irregular crystals
⟁				Graupel
△•				Sleet
▲				Hail

precipitation never reaches the Earth because it melts as it enters the lower, warmer air. Hailstones, though, frequently reach the ground even at hot temperatures.

Precipitation that evaporates before reaching the ground is called virga.

Snow. The crystalline nature of snow allows it to assume many forms, reflecting the temperature and moisture conditions in the supercooled clouds in which the particles form. The density of freshly fallen snow is about $\frac{1}{10}$ that of liquid water. Wetter and warmer varieties of frozen precipitation, especially sleet and graupel, may be half as dense as liquid water.

Graupel. Sometimes called soft hail or snow grains, graupel consists primarily of a mass of frozen cloud droplets. If the initial particle is a cluster of ice needles, the graupel tends to have a conical form. If the initial particle is an aggregation of cloud droplets, the graupel appears as a lumpy, somewhat spherical particle.

Graupel is soft. When a graupel particle hits an object it often flattens out into a rounded spot of powdery snow with no apparent crystalline structure.

Graupel often forms in strong updrafts of cold air and in blizzards and snowstorms occurring downwind of a lake. The particles are often highly electrified. Graupel is often found in severe lightning storms and frequently serves as the core of a hailstone. The particles are 1–7 mm in diameter.

Sleet. The rattle of sleet on the windowpane is a familiar sound during a freezing rain. Sleet particles often have a curious structure. As drizzle rain falls into cold air, it freezes from the outside inward. Just before the drop is completely frozen, the interior water, expanding with great force as it freezes, cracks the ice sphere and flows to the surface, where it freezes in the form of a tiny ice needle. Some other partly frozen drops may break open when they hit the ground, leaving cuplike fragments. Other drops may combine with ice crystals or transform them to lumpy, transparent ice fragments.

SOLID PRECIPITATION, cont.

Rime. When supercooled clouds sweep over a mountain summit, the cloud droplets often freeze on impact with exposed objects. This produces rime, substantial ice-feather formations that grow into the wind. Rime formations may be very grainy if the drops freeze instantly, or very smooth if the cloud water has a chance to flow before it solidifies. The stronger the wind and the larger the supercooled cloud droplets, the larger and more rapid the rime formation. Structures up to a meter long commonly form on trees and other objects on mountaintops.

Hail. This form of frozen precipitation causes the greatest damage. Hail particles form in the cores of large cumulonimbus clouds and may grow to a maximum size within a small region of intensive updraft. This region, called the accumulation zone, can contain 10 grams or more per cubic meter of liquid and ice crystals. Within this zone the particle's increasing weight is balanced by an ever-increasing upward air velocity.

Hoar frost is an opaque, granular deposit of ice formed when supercooled cloud droplets freeze rapidly after hitting an exposed object such as a mountaintop branch.

At times a hailstone may start falling only to encounter a new and more intense updraft that will carry it even higher into the clouds, and perhaps even toss it out the top so that it falls to Earth through clear air. Or a hailstone may fall through the cloud as the updraft weakens, sweeping up more droplets and ice crystals until it leaves the cloud.

In cross section, a large hailstone looks like an onion with transparent and translucent layers. Photographing a thin section of a hailstone with polarized light (see photo) shows that the stone consists of crystalline bits ranging in size from 10 to 2000 microns. These units indicate periods of wet and dry growth. The larger crystals form during wet growth, as the hailstone partially melts and then refreezes, and the smaller elements represent frozen cloud droplets and ice crystals cemented together by moisture during dry growth. The opaque ice is caused by tiny, trapped air bubbles.

Hailstones that have partially melted and then refrozen while falling may have a diameter of 10 mm or more and, if melted, will produce splash marks on impact 3 cm or more in diameter. Hailstones can sometimes grow to the size of a small grapefruit.

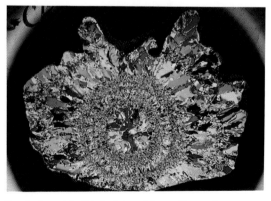

Two inches wide, this hailstone fell on a Kansas farm in June 1969. This thin section was photographed using two crossed polarizing filters.

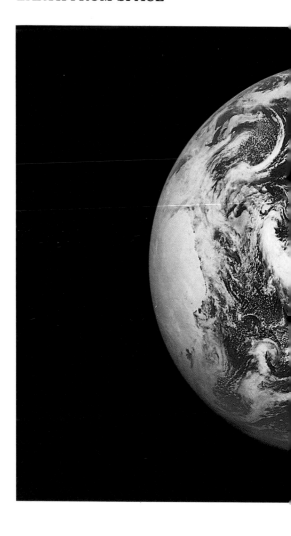

When photographs like these first began to come back from Earth orbiter missions, people were amazed by the beauty of our planet. In this picture, taken in 1972 from *Apollo 17*, the continent of Africa is clearly visible. This was the first Apollo trajectory from which it was possible to photograph the South Polar icecap, at left.

WEATHER SATELLITES

The satellite that created this photo of a large cloud system is one of five geostationary weather satellites. A geostationary satellite is positioned high over the equator and orbits at the same rate the Earth rotates. Each satellite monitors the large area between 55°N and 55°S. Other satellites in a north-south orbit provide sharp images of the polar regions.

COLD FRONTS

Think of a box filled with air. The density, or mass per unit volume, of the air is determined by the mass of each molecule and by the number of the molecules. More slow-moving molecules can be packed into the box than fast-moving molecules. In other words, cold air is denser than warm air, since coldness means slower molecular movement.

Gravity holds the densest air closest to the Earth's surface. It follows that a cold air mass will run under a warmer air mass in its path, causing the warmer air to rise.

A cold front is the boundary along which an advancing mass of cold air displaces a warmer air mass.

Because of the abrupt uplift given to the warm and moist air, cold fronts are often associated with a line of cumulonimbus clouds.

A cross section of a cold front is shown below. Keep in mind that the atmosphere is very thin compared to the Earth's radius, 40 miles to 4000 — as the peach skin is to the peach. It would be difficult to draw a cross-section diagram true to scale, so the vertical dimension is exaggerated.

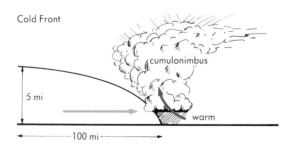

Cold Front

cumulonimbus

5 mi

warm

← 100 mi →

Cumulonimbus clouds and showers often form at the leading edge of a cold air mass, called a cold front.

WARM FRONTS

If a warm air mass is moving faster than a retreating cold air mass, the warm, less dense
air will ride over the cold air. The boundary
along which this occurs is called a warm front.

The slope of the warm front is more gentle
than that of the cold front. As a result, the ascent is less abrupt and produces a layered sequence of clouds that range (high to low) from
cirrostratus to altostratus to nimbostratus.

The cause of the difference in the slopes of
warm and cold fronts can be seen by doing the
simple experiment shown in the figure below.
Hold a pencil with the eraser touching a table
or desk. Push or pull the pencil. The slowing
effect of surface friction causes the slope of the
pencil to increase in the case of a push (as
with advancing cold air) and decrease in the
case of a pull (as with a retreating cool air
mass).

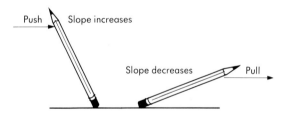

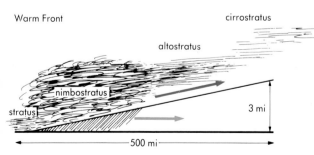

Stratus clouds form as a warm air mass rides up over a retreating cool air mass.

THE WAVE CYCLONE

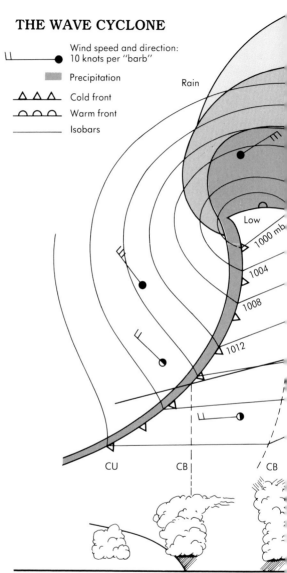

Wind speed and direction:
10 knots per "barb"

Precipitation

△△△ Cold front

◠◠◠ Warm front

Isobars

Rain

Low

1000 mb

1004

1008

1012

CU   CB   CB

The wave cyclone model shows how Nature moves excess
heat energy from low latitudes to high. In the Northern
Hemisphere, warm air is transported north and cold air
south. A wave at the boundary of air masses of different

106

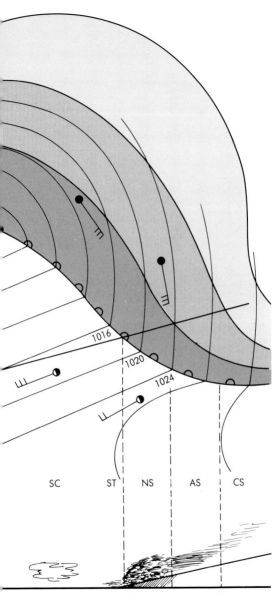

densities, moving generally from west to east, is born, grows
to maturity, and dies. Becoming familiar with the distribution of various weather elements in the wave cyclone is an
important step in learning single-station forecasting.

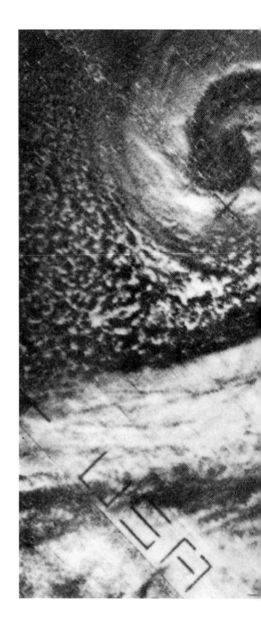

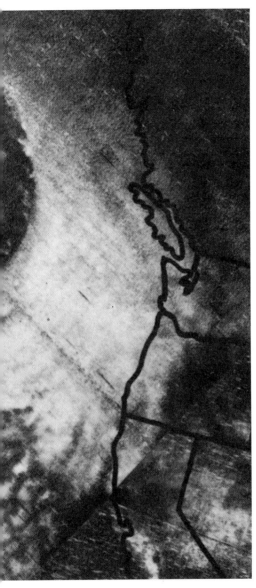

An early weather satellite photographed this classic example of a deeply occluded, high-latitude wave cyclone in 1967. Note the positions of the surface fronts (see pp. 106-107).

WEATHER MAPS

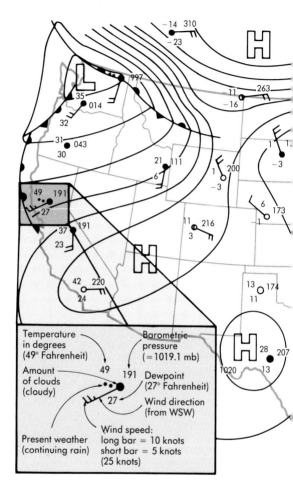

The Daily Weather Maps issued by the National Weather Service summarize the data gathered at weather stations all around the country. The data from each station are displayed in a *station model*. Station models contain an amazing amount of information in a tiny space (see the key). Meteorologists analyze all this information, then plot the isobars and frontal positions.

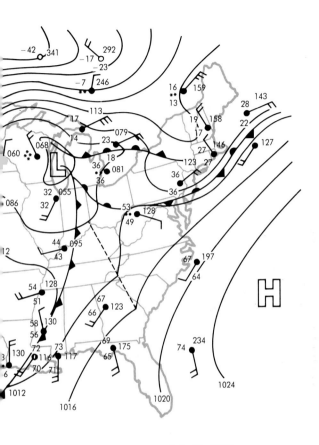

Feb. 16, 1990

VISIBILITY

The song title goes, "On a clear day you can see forever." Unfortunately, on this increasingly crowded planet that is rarely true. The lower atmosphere is loaded with small particles from wind-driven dust, forest fires, volcanic eruptions, and breaking waves.

In addition, there are increasing numbers of particles introduced from industrial smokestacks, home chimneys, automobile and airplane exhaust, landfills, etc.

The situation can become critical in a populous town located in a bowl or valley during a period of stable air. Particles and gaseous emissions have no place to go. They accumulate and may build up to health-threatening levels. The last great air pollution incident in this country took place in Donora, Pa., in October 1948. Forty-three percent of the population were adversely affected, and 20 people died.

Fortunately, precipitation is a natural air cleaner. When rain falls through the atmosphere, small pollution particles are caught up by the raindrops and are carried to Earth.

When new, unstable air masses move into a region, there can be mixing and overturning, with dramatic improvements in visibility.

Denver, Colo. is sited in a basin at the foot of the Rocky Mountains. A stable atmosphere can lead to severe air pollution, above. At right, Denver on a clear day. Pikes Peak, 75 miles distant, is clearly visible.

112

STABILITY AND CLOUDINESS

One of the most important factors shaping the weather is the stability of the atmosphere. If the atmosphere is stable, air parcels will return to their original positions after vertical displacement. If the atmosphere is unstable, however, upward motions are encouraged.

The stability of the atmosphere is the cause of the two basic cloud types: stratus clouds form in a stable atmosphere; cumulus clouds form in an unstable atmosphere.

On the whole, the atmosphere is quite stable, and its predominant motion is horizontal. An air mass may move horizontally many thousands of miles, while the air within the mass may not move upward more than a mile.

When an air mass moves over a warmer surface, it is heated and becomes unstable. The lower levels become less dense and are then buoyed up. This initiates a sequence of events described in the Precipitation Ladder.

Conversely, air moving over a colder surface is cooled, and it becomes denser and more stable. Surface cooling may lead to fog. If air is lifted over hills or warm fronts, widespread layer clouds such as altostratus and nimbostratus may be produced.

Cumulus clouds are always separated heaps because the rising air in the cloud mass is always compensated by adjacent sinking air, and sinking air inhibits cloud formation.

WIND AND PRESSURE

Air pressure, the weight of the atmosphere on a unit area such as a square centimeter, is measured by meteorologists in units called millibars. The average air pressure at sea level is 1013 millibars. But it continually changes from time to time and place to place. It is these changes that cause the wind.

On a weather map, areas of equal pressure are connected by lines called isobars, just as topographic maps display contour lines of equal elevation.

Like everything that has mass, air is pulled downward by gravity, which causes it to move across the isobars from high to low pressure. The greater the pressure gradient — that is, the more closely spaced the isobars — the stronger the pull of gravity, and the faster the winds.

The Earth rotates out from under the moving air (except at the equator), introducing another factor, the Coriolis effect. When the pressure gradient force and the Coriolis force of the Earth's rotation are balanced, the wind blows parallel to the isobars so that, if you stand with your back to the wind, high pressure is to your right and low pressure is to your left, in the Northern Hemisphere.

Generally, air moves clockwise around high pressure systems and counterclockwise around low-pressure systems. The reverse is true in the Southern Hemisphere because of the reversed Coriolis effect.

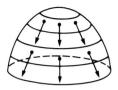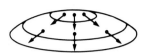

On a non-rotating Earth, gravity would pull air directly from high- to low-pressure areas, causing "hills" of high air pressure to flatten *(above)*. But the Earth rotates out from under its atmosphere, introducing an effect called the Coriolis Force *(below)*, which pulls air to the right in the Northern Hemisphere, left in the Southern Hemisphere. When the forces of the pressure gradient (PGF) and the Coriolis Force (CF) are balanced, the wind blows parallel to the isobars, producing clockwise circulation about high-pressure areas and counterclockwise circulation about lows (vice versa in the Southern Hemisphere). The effects of centripetal force are not shown in this illustration.

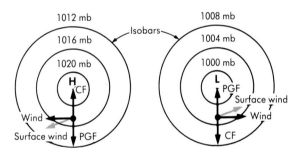

TROUGHS AND RIDGES

If we could see the atmosphere from above, looking down on either the North or South Pole we would see a vortex, or swirl, of high-speed winds. The winds move from west to east, faster than Earth rotates below.

Superimposed on the west winds are waves or ripples, like those that form in a twitched rope. As you can see in the illustration below, the ripples are three-dimensional, with north-south movements and vertical (up-down) movements.

These ripples are shown in the meteorologists' important "half the atmosphere" chart. The chart shows the elevation of a surface on which the pressure is 500 millibars, or roughly half the standard air pressure.

The 500-millibar surface slopes downhill from the equator to the poles, ranging from about 19,000 ft. (5.8 km) at the equator to about 16,000 ft. (4.9 km) at the poles. The slope is steeper in winter. Ridges and troughs have the same meaning as on topographic maps, i.e., ridges are areas of high elevation (and pressure), and troughs are areas of low elevation (and pressure). The 500-millibar

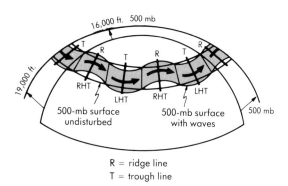

R = ridge line
T = trough line

A typical pattern of troughs and ridges in the upper-level westerly winds.

chart shows the steering pattern of storms and is very useful in making weather forecasts.

The illustration below shows a typical pattern of waves in the westerly winds. Imagine skating along the lines with your back to the wind. Where there is a right-hand turning of the winds (RHT) you would be farthest north and highest. Where there is a left-hand turning (LHT) you would be farthest south and lowest. RHT is associated with sinking air; LHT with rising air. Regions of rising air are regions of cloudiness and precipitation; regions of descending air are regions of clear skies. Surface fronts generally are found under the trough regions.

Jet stream

When upper-level cold, polar air moves south, and warm, tropical air moves north, the result is the formation of a band along which there is rapid transition from cold to warm. A ribbon, or current, of very rapidly moving air develops here, sometimes reaching speeds of 200 mph (320 kph) or more, but more commonly in the 100–150 mph (160–240 kph) range. This is called the jet stream. Storm centers are steered by the jet stream so it is of great importance to weather-watchers. The jet stream is stronger in winter than in summer because temperature contrasts are greater in that season.

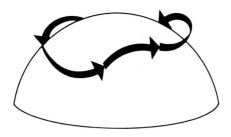

The jet stream is a core of high-speed winds (200 mph or more) embedded in the westerly winds. Pilots headed east can dramatically increase their speed by flying in the jet stream.

LEARNING TO FORECAST

What will the weather be like today, or tomorrow? We all ask these questions, because the weather affects our lives — our activities, what clothes we will wear, whether we will walk or take the bus.

Professional forecasters gather vast amounts of weather information, but they still are unable to make forecasts that are 100 percent accurate because the problem is too complex. You probably don't have professional technology at hand, but you can still attempt valid forecasts using just your own observations.

Every locale has its weather sage, a person known for his or her ability to tell what tomorrow's weather will be. These people are skilled observers of the near sky and have built up a body of experience about the causes of weather. They know that when certain conditions of wind, humidity, temperature, and cloud exist, then certain weather consequences will follow. The key is skilled observation, and the ability is acquired only by practice.

A good starting point is to become familiar with the wave cyclone model (pp. 106–107). Study the different clouds associated with various parts of the cyclone and the wind and temperature distribution. For instance, the combination of southeasterly winds, falling barometer readings, and increasing cirrostratus clouds with a halo are good indicators of steady rain within 48 hours.

Of course, the wave cyclone model is only a starting point. It will need modification depending on where you live. Weather in Oregon is different from that in Virginia, or New York, or Honolulu.

ACTIVITY

Observing the weather

If you want to engage in a hobby that will capture your interest for a lifetime, try observing and recording the weather every day. The chart below shows one way you could record your weather observations.

One useful way to gain practice is to set yourself a contest with your favorite local television weatherperson. Write down your own forecast, then write down the TV forecast. Compare them; analyze your mistakes. Sometimes (but not often) your forecast may be the more accurate one.

	Day 1	Day 2	Day 3	Day 4
State of sky	◔	◕	●	
Wind direction and speed	NW LT.	N LT.	SE Mod.	
Max. temp.	60	56	65	
Min. Temp.	50	46	58	
Barometer	29.94	30.03	29.90	
24 h. Precip. inches	0.10	—	—	
Precip. kind	Shwrs	—	—	
Clouds (low)	Cu	Cu	—	
clouds (middle)	—	—	Ac	
clouds (high)	few Ci	—	Cs	
Remarks	Shwrs early in period	clearing	Increasing clouds	

ACTIVITY

Making a cloud atlas

This book is principally about clouds and is itself a sort of cloud atlas. You can supplement the pictures in this book with ones you find in various publications or ones you paint, draw, or photograph yourself. Your atlas will expand over time, and you will find that you learn a lot by being both information gatherer and editor.

Here is how to go about it: Get a large three-ring binder with dividers. Label the tabs using the organization scheme in this book. Include sections for unusual or complex clouds, for the sky frequently is a mix of different types.

Good sources of cloudscapes will be found in state public-relations magazines such as *Arizona Highways.* Also look at travel brochures and magazines such as *National Geographic.* Cut out the pictures (if permissible), label and store them until a "rainy day" when you can mount them in the proper sections.

Cloud photography is a challenging and satisfying hobby. You don't have to have fancy camera equipment to get started. Use a polarizing filter if your camera will accept it. This will improve your photos by filtering out glare and enhancing the blue of the sky. Hold your camera very still when snapping the photo. Frame the picture carefully to eliminate foreground clutter. Photograph mainly in the morning and evening hours. Think of yourself as wearing two hats simultaneously: that of scientist and that of artist.

ACTIVITY

Check-off list for observing clouds

If you are a new cloud observer, we recommend that you photocopy this page and use it to help you identify a cloud type. Go through the steps and check off the blanks that apply. Soon you will be able to use this systematic approach to observing and classifying clouds mentally and, in due time, it will become a habit.

Step 1. Clouds are mainly
_____ separated heaps
_____ layers
_____ precipitating

Step 2. If precipitating
_____ steadily, with light to medium
          intensity, then: **Nimbostratus**
_____ intermittently, with medium to heavy
          intensity, then: **Cumulonimbus**
_____ trails of ice crystals not reaching
          ground, then: **Cirrus**

Step 3. If heap only, top is
H _____   **Cumulus Congestus**
M _____   **Swelling Cumulus**
L _____   **Fair-weather Cumulus**

Step 4. If layer only,
Base   Top
H _____ _____   **Cirrostratus**
M _____ _____   **Altostratus**
L _____ _____   **Stratus**

Step 5. If mix of heaps and layers,
Base   Top
H _____ _____   **Cirrocumulus**
M _____ _____   **Altocumulus**
L _____ _____   **Stratocumulus**

L = 0–10,000 ft.
M = 10,000–25,000 ft.
H = 25,000–50,000 ft.

Epilogue

As we move into the last decade of this century, our awareness is growing that mankind's activity is imperiling Earth's atmosphere. The world's population continues to explode, and the negative impact will increase dramatically unless certain practices that are now accepted as normal are radically changed.

We must move toward a sustainable society in which there is a balance between livability and livelihood. Our convenience-oriented, industrialized, throwaway society has been too little concerned with the negative impact of its actions. This has led to three major concerns for the atmosphere: acid rain, ozone depletion, and global warming.

Acid rain. Earlier we mentioned the benefits of periodic washing of the atmosphere by rain. But now the atmosphere contains acidic pollutants released by factories and cars, and there is a dark side of this washing: the impact that acidic raindrops have on lakes and forests. Acidic runoff leaves some lakes so acid that they are no longer able to support fish populations. Trees watered by acidic rain wither and die. These effects are particularly felt downwind of large industrial establishments.

Ozone depletion. At the top of the atmosphere, a shell of ozone shields Earth against the very energetic ultraviolet rays of the solar spectrum. Ozone is a compound of three oxygen atoms, unlike the normal oxygen molecule (O_2) that we breathe.

Studies seem to show that the ozone layer is being depleted, with "holes," or thinning of the ozone layer, first showing up over Antarctica in the late 1970s. The culprit seems to be chlorofluorocarbons (CFCs). CFCs are used in refrigerators, air conditioners, and industrial solvents. They are used in making insulation and polystyrene foam, the plastic in which some fast-food restaurants serve sandwiches and coffee. CFCs are stable, long-lived compounds that slowly work their way up to the stratosphere, where solar ultraviolet light

122

breaks them apart. This frees a chlorine atom that catalyzes a reaction with the ozone molecules, converting them to oxygen, which offers no ultraviolet protection. One CFC molecule may cause the destruction of as many as 100,000 ozone molecules.

Were we to stop all use of CFCs, those now present would continue the work of destruction for decades. Worldwide use of CFCs would have to be reduced immediately by half to stabilize their concentration to today's level.

Global warming. Carbon dioxide in the atmosphere traps long-wave infrared radiation. This is the cause of the "greenhouse effect" that has made Earth a climatic paradise with a warm, moist environment — quite in contrast with our closest neighbors, Mars (too cold) and Venus (too hot).

But the amount of carbon dioxide in the atmosphere has increased by about 25% in the last century and continues to build up at an increasing rate. This is mainly the result of Earth's booming population and the attendant

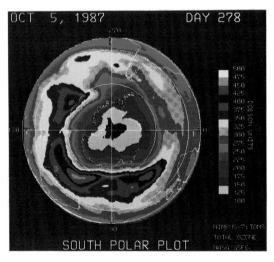

This computer-colored photograph shows the "hole" in the ozone layer over Antarctica. The color bar at right shows the relative concentrations of ozone.

EPILOGUE, cont.

increased burning of fossil fuels (coal, oil, and gas) in home heating, transportation, and industrial processing. Other "greenhouse gases," including oxides of nitrogen, CFCs, and methane, are also increasing rapidly. The net effect is global warming, but how much, how fast, what its impact will be, and how we will cope with them are questions that are still unanswered.

Atmospheric scientists use computer models to forecast conditions days, months, even years in the future. But the longer-range the projection, the less reliable the forecast. The sun-atmosphere-Earth-ocean system is just too complex. If Earth's average surface temperature increases by about 5°F, as suggested by several models of global warming, there will be resultant climatic changes — but we are unable to predict with any certainty what they may be.

If there is a substantial change in patterns of rainfall distribution, farmlands may become unworkable. If ocean levels rise, major seaports could be wiped out. Society will have to adapt, and the social costs will be enormous.

Will we act now, before scientific judgment is rendered with unanimity? Or will we wait to initiate social action and risk the fatal trap of "too little, too late"? We suggest that global warming is a "both/and" issue rather than one of "either/or."

We do hope that this book will play a role in increasing the awareness of its readers so that they will take actions, be they ever so small, to protect the atmosphere of Earth, our precious home.

Acknowledgments

A special word of thanks to Vincent Schaefer, who in 1971 invited me to assist in the writing of *Peterson's Field Guide to the Atmosphere*. Many good things have flowed from this connection. I wish also to acknowledge Jack Borden, founder of For Spacious Skies, an organization that seeks to stimulate an awareness of the beauty of the skies. Teachers can order the FSS Cloud Chart and Activity Guide from 54 Webb St., Lexington, MA 01273.

Thanks are due several persons in the scientific community who have said "yes" to my request for special pictures. Thay are: (Mrs.) Carl Anderson, p. 40 (bottom); Bob Day, p. 41 (top); Joseph Golden at NOAA, p. 53 (bottom); George Haltiner, p. 50 (top); Bob Henry, p. 55 (top); Charles Knight, p. 99; David Lynch, p. 77 (top); Edi Ann Otto, p. 53 (top); Pekka Parviainen, pp. 5, 48 (bottom), 65 (bottom); Terry Peasley, p. 75 (bottom); Sherill Roberts, p. 58 (top); and of course Vincent Schaefer, pp. 27 (top), 31 (both), 33 (top), 35 (top), 41 (bottom), 42 (bottom), 45 (bottom), 49 (top), 50 (bottom), 55 (bottom), 56 (top), 57 (top), 73 (bottom), 75 (top), 77 (bottom), and 93 (bottom). Thanks also to the Colorado Dept. of Health, pp. 112–113; NASA, pp. 6–7, 52 (top), 57 (bottom), 58 (bottom), 59 (both), 100–101, 123; NOAA, pp. 53 (bottom), 102–103; and NSSL, pp. 34, 51 (both). To former student Jeanne Neff, thanks again for capturing the "flying saucer" (cover and p. 42, top) and for giving me permission to use the photo.

Special thanks to Mary Reilly, who executed the diagrams; to Christy Day Leonhardt, who drew the originals from which some of the diagrams were adapted; and to Anne Chalmers, who drew the diagram of the water cycle. Thanks also to Ruth and Wesley Caspers, to former colleague of Fred Decker of the Weather Workbook, and to Susan Kunhardt of Houghton Mifflin.

And to Mary, my dear wife of 53 years, my appreciation for forbearance and love.

John A. Day

Index

Page numbers in **bold** indicate illustrations.

127